TWO DIALOGUES ON DHAMMA

Bhikkhu Nyanasobhano

BUDDHIST PUBLICATION SOCIETY
KANDY,   SRI LANKA

Buddhist Publication Society
P.O. Box 61
54, Sangharaja Mawatha
Kandy, Sri Lanka

Copyright © 1989 by Bhikkhu Nyanasobhano
All rights reserved

ISBN 955-24-0057-0

Offset in Sri Lanka by
Karunaratne & Sons Ltd.
647, Kularatne Mawatha
Colombo 10

BHIKKHU TISSA MEETS A SKEPTIC

Outside a Buddhist temple, early on a summer Saturday morning, a monk named Bhikkhu Tissa is sweeping the stone walk. His work is neither slow nor fast, but steady and careful, as if the sweeping of dust and leaves were something important to him. From the road some yards away comes the hum of an approaching automobile. In the morning quiet the hum rises to a rumble, and a shiny sports car passes by. If Bhikkhu Tissa were watching—which he is not—he would notice that the driver momentarily slows down and regards him curiously before disappearing around a curve. Then there is a slight screech of tires and in a moment the sports car returns and zooms into the driveway by the temple. Mr. Carp, a young man in expensive, casual clothes, climbs out and approaches the monk.

MR. CARP: Hey there, friend.
BHIKKHU TISSA: Good morning.
CARP: My name's Carp. I'm a friend of Charlie Prentice. You know him, I think?
BHIKKHU: Oh yes, Mr. Prentice comes by quite often now.
CARP: You are Bhikkhu Tissa, aren't you?
BHIKKHU: Yes, I am.

CARP: Or *Venerable* Tissa, Charlie says. You guys sure have some strange names.

BHIKKHU: Is there anything I can do for you, Mr. Carp?

CARP: Probably not, to tell the truth. I'm on my way down to the beach, and anyway I'm not really interested in Buddhism. But I was reading these books, see.

BHIKKHU: Books on Buddhism?

CARP: Yes.

BHIKKHU: Why were you reading books on Buddhism if you're not interested in it? It sounds like a terrible waste of time.

CARP: Well, I mean—maybe it was! Charlie gave me those books, and let me tell you they were pretty annoying. All that talk about *suffering*. I mean, page after page of misery, old age, death, and so on. It sounds like Buddhism is the most pessimistic religion in the world. I got to thinking about it, and I was wondering why you Buddhists have such a negative attitude toward life and why you dwell on suffering.

BHIKKHU (Musing): You might also say that suffering dwells on *us*.

CARP: How's that? Anyhow, I saw you just now, and I thought, why not ask the guy about it? So I have a few questions. Unless you're busy, of course.

BHIKKHU (Smiling, leaning the broom against a wall): I'd be glad to try to answer questions about the Dhamma.

CARP: "Dhamma." That's the word that keeps popping up in those books. What does it mean? I forget.

BHIKKHU: Usually it means just the teaching of the Buddha. It also means truth, reality, the way things are, the law of the universe, bare phenomena themselves, the path to deliverance—depending on the context.

CARP: It's pretty important, huh?

BHIKKHU: The word is just a word. What's behind the word is the most important thing in the world.

CARP: I figured you'd say something like that. I'd like to hear about it. Say, could we sit down somewhere?

BHIKKHU: Sure. How about this nice patch of grass over here?

CARP (With an attempt at humor): I guess you don't have any lawn chairs around here!

BHIKKHU: We make do with what we have. I find grass very accommodating.

(They sit down in a shady spot. Mr. Carp uncomfortably inspects the area for ants.)

CARP: You know, Bhikkhu Tissa, I never met a Buddhist monk before. I understand people treat you monks with all kinds of respect.

BHIKKHU: Depends on the person, depends on the monk.

CARP: You get called "venerable sir" and all that.

BHIKKHU: We get called other things too.

CARP: Yes, I bet you do! But let me get on to my questions. This business of suffering really bothers me. Isn't there enough trouble in the world without you Buddhists harping on it?

BHIKKHU: It's precisely *because* there is trouble in the world that we pay attention to it, or harp on it, if you will.

CARP: Do you think you can do anything about it?

BHIKKHU: Yes. That's the reason Buddhism exists.

CARP: This I want to hear. To me, it seems like we should emphasize the happy side of life. Why should we pay attention to all the misery?

BHIKKHU: If a wasp stings you, do you pay attention to it?

CARP: Well, of course.

BHIKKHU: But what good does that do? Why dwell on it?

CARP: Because I want to get away from it, because I don't want to be stung again.

BHIKKHU: If you don't want to be stung again it would make sense to learn something about wasps, wouldn't it? Where they build their nests, what's likely to upset them, how to keep from annoying them, and so on. There are a great many kinds of suffering in the world, and they all have their own causes and characteristics. If you feel any of these afflictions, or think that you might be prey to them, wouldn't it be wise to take a good look at them and see what might be done about them?

CARP: Yes, that's so, I suppose. But any way you go there's some amount of trouble, so I prefer to accent the positive, so to speak. You've got to take the bitter with the sweet!

Bhikkhu Tissa Meets a Skeptic 5

BHIKKHU: Would I be wrong in guessing that you have a fair amount of "sweet" in your life?

CARP: It's true, I'm getting along real well. I work for a real estate development company, organizing some new projects. And to tell the truth, I'm doing pretty well at it. Life's good to me, I admit. That's why I object to Buddhism.

BHIKKHU: Are you completely satisfied with the way things are?

CARP: Not completely. Who is? The important thing is to keep totally in command of your life.

BHIKKHU: Permit me to disagree. Nobody keeps totally in command of his life. Consider just your body. You look pretty healthy. But can you keep your body from ever getting sick? Can you keep it from getting old and breaking down? Or from dying?

CARP: No, I can't do that.

BHIKKHU: Or consider your work. Can you be sure your colleagues will treat you fairly?

CARP (Grunting): Those guys? No way!

BHIKKHU: Will your creditors always be tolerant? Will your customers always pay their bills quickly? Will your competitors put up no resistance?

CARP (Uncomfortably): There's a lot of uncertainty in business.

BHIKKHU: There's a lot of uncertainty in social life, in family life, in all spheres of activity. Am I wrong? What do you think?

CARP: No, I can't deny it.

BHIKKHU: Or, to get right down to the most

important thing, can you keep totally in control of your own mind?

CARP: I'm a pretty cheerful guy.

BHIKKHU: That's not what I asked, Mr. Carp. When things go wrong around you, can you keep your mind steady and peaceful?

CARP: Of course not. How could that be?

BHIKKHU: If you tell your mind not to get upset or angry or distracted, does it obey you?

CARP: That's a funny way to look at it. But no, I guess my mind pretty much does what it likes. Thoughts and feelings just come boiling up.

BHIKKHU: Then you certainly aren't in command of your mind, are you? And if you can't control your body or your mind or the actions of other people, you can hardly say you're in command of your life.

CARP: It was just a figure of speech.

BHIKKHU: Let's examine this a bit further, if you don't mind. How many people, do you think, can control their lives to *any* degree?

CARP: Not many probably. You never know what will happen.

BHIKKHU: Right. You never know what will happen. If it's pleasant you will be elated. If it's unpleasant you will be upset and depressed. If someone is kind to you, you'll be gratified. If they cheat you, you'll be angry. Tell me, Mr. Carp, do you see any independence or security in this state of affairs?

CARP: Since you put it like that, not much. I suppose we have to admit we live in insecurity and dependence to a large degree.

BHIKKHU: Would you call this situation pleasant or unpleasant?

CARP: Unpleasant, mostly.

BHIKKHU: The Buddha spoke about sorrow, pain, and insecurity not because he *liked* them but because he saw them as the key to an understanding of life.

CARP: Pessimistic, like I say.

BHIKKHU: A fact is just a fact. If you're going to come to a good decision about how to act, you need accurate information about the matter at hand. So you look, and you take note of the important details you see, regardless of whether or not they are personally appealing to you.

CARP: What was the Buddha looking for?

BHIKKHU: Ah! A good question. He was looking for a way out.

CARP: A way out of ... dependence and insecurity?

BHIKKHU: Exactly. The word that describes this situation is *dukkha*. This is usually translated as "suffering," but it means a great deal more than that. "Unsatisfactoriness" might be a better word.

CARP: Well, excuse me, Bhikkhu Tissa, but when you get right down to it, *everything* is unsatisfactory to some degree.

BHIKKHU: Indeed?

CARP: Nothing is *completely* dependable. You can't expect that. Everything has flaws.

BHIKKHU: How about permanent? Are pleasure and security permanent?

CARP: Not in my experience. You've got to keep chasing them down. That's what life is all about.

BHIKKHU: Let's see if I can summarize a bit. Nobody—at least, nobody that we know of—can truly control his own body and make it do exactly what he wants. Nobody can tell his mind how to behave when disturbing events occur. Nobody can prevent disasters from happening to him or keep people from doing things he doesn't like. Nobody can make pleasures last or keep good feelings from fading away. So we find ourselves always running after something desirable or away from something frightful. What would you call this state of affairs?

(There is a pause while Mr. Carp fidgets, plucks grass blades, laughs.)

CARP: Suffering. Okay, suffering or unsatisfactoriness or whatever you want to call it. It goes pretty deep, does it?

BHIKKHU: It is stitched right into the fabric of things. You could even say it's the thread in the fabric itself.

CARP: What a view of life! Now, let me ask, the Buddha was looking for a way out. And he found it, I suppose?

BHIKKHU: He did. The way out that he found is called Dhamma, the word we began with.

CARP: So this Dhamma that the Buddha created can get us out of suffering?

BHIKKHU: The Buddha didn't create it. He only discovered it and made it known. The Dhamma exists whether or not anybody knows it or understands it, just as apples will continue to fall from trees whether or not anyone understands the law of gravity.

CARP: Is Dhamma some kind of god?

BHIKKHU: No. The Dhamma has many aspects, but basically it is just the way things are, the underlying laws of the universe.

CARP: That sounds simple enough. Why isn't it self-evident, then? Why don't people recognize it?

BHIKKHU: Suppose on a dangerous seacoast there were a powerful light, a great beacon in a lighthouse. Would that be self-evident to sailors?

CARP: Certainly.

BHIKKHU: But what if the sailors never came out of their cabins, or had the odd habit of wearing heavy cloths over their heads, or slept all the time?

CARP: They wouldn't see it, then. They would run aground. But what kind of metaphor are you suggesting?

BHIKKHU: Fundamental truth, or Dhamma, is not by its nature hidden or obscure, though countless philosophers have thought so. But there is something that prevents us from seeing the Dhamma. It is called ignorance. This ignorance, this not-knowing, this blankness, covers our minds and distorts our view of reality. The sailors in the ship may never leave the cabin—they may remain simply sunk in ignorance without trying to get out. Or they may intentionally blind themselves with the masks of foolish beliefs and delusions. Or they may sleep all the time, out of laziness and stupidity. So they will not see the light and may even deny that any such thing exists.

CARP: But suppose somebody does see this Dhamma, or sees enough of it to know it's a good thing.

BHIKKHU: Then, if he's sensible, he'll follow it, he'll seek its protection.

CARP: But what kind of protection can Dhamma offer against all this suffering and uncertainty we were just talking about?

BHIKKHU: Above all, the Dhamma offers relief. There is relief from doubt, relief from fear, relief from mental anguish, relief from grief. As we study and practise Dhamma, our ignorance about how the universe works is gradually reduced. We begin to understand cause and effect. We see that certain results follow from certain actions and we learn to govern our actions in order to get happy results. So we gain relief from doubt and begin to have confidence in our ability to make sense of the world. Right now, we may be subject to all kinds of fears about what may happen to us, thinking that some terrible fate may come crashing down on us at any moment. But the Dhamma teaches us that fear is one result of clinging to a permanence that does not really exist. When we are reconciled to the always-changing nature of things, fear can be overcome. Also, we gain relief from mental anguish, another result of clinging and craving, because we train our minds according to Dhamma merely to pay attention to events and objects, not to clutch them as "me" or "mine." If we have no obsession with being a "sufferer," then the suffering itself loses force. Then, as for grief, we have less to endure because we learn that all life is a constant flow and that grief is, in a sense, simply our own unhappy invention. To know how life works is a great protection, because it gives us confidence and helps us avoid suffering.

CARP: These are big promises, Bhikkhu Tissa!

BHIKKHU: These are just possibilities, very real possibilities—but not things that will happen simply because someone calls himself a Buddhist. I don't expect you to believe them.

CARP: You don't?

BHIKKHU: Certainly not. Buddhism holds out great hope to mankind but it does not expect or advise people to believe a set of doctrines without confirmation.

CARP: And what kind of confirmation is necessary?

BHIKKHU: Why, the confirmation of your own mind, your own reason, your own experience. Could anything less satisfy you?

CARP: Well, I believe in my own experience, all right. But why do you bother to tell me about these benefits of the Dhamma?

BHIKKHU: There is a saying that Buddhas only point the way. The Buddha doesn't "save" anybody. He only teaches people how to save themselves. He points out the problems of life and shows how they may be solved. We who are followers of the Buddha try to observe the same principle—we try to point out the way and encourage people to make the journey for themselves.

CARP: So you think that if people will make this journey they will find confirmation of Buddhist teachings for themselves?

BHIKKHU: Yes. You see, the truths the Buddha points out are right here in the body and the mind. Anyone can see them who puts his mind to it, but he has to put his mind to it.

CARP: Can you explain some of these truths? I assure you there's no danger of my believing them without proof!

BHIKKHU: We've already touched on the truth of suffering. As we've noted, suffering or unsatisfactoriness is present in all worldly phenomena to one degree or another. This is one characteristic of existence that the Buddha repeatedly emphasizes. Then there is the fact of impermanence.

CARP: Well, nothing lasts forever. Sure, I know that.

BHIKKHU: Excuse me, but the mark of *aniccatā* or impermanence is extremely deep. Anybody can notice gross physical changes—and these are certainly one aspect of impermanence—but few people realize that *everything* that exists in the world is whirling in a blur of change, rising and falling every second, flashing in and out of existence, being born and dying, appearing and perishing continually.

CARP: You know, modern physicists describe atoms and sub-atomic particles in almost the same way—as changing with incredible speed all the time.

BHIKKHU: So they do. But it's not necessary to

study physics to understand this. The best laboratory is the mind itself. Have you ever known anything to change faster than your own mind?

CARP: Sometimes I think my head will bust wide open, the way my thoughts run on!

BHIKKHU: Sometimes faster and wilder than you would wish?

CARP: I suppose I've already admitted I don't have much control over my mind. Sometimes it's just a storm of passions, ideas, emotions, memories.

BHIKKHU: Can you remember a time when it wasn't like this?

CARP: No, and that's pretty depressing.

BHIKKHU: It's simply the nature of the mind. Part of our trouble comes from conceiving the notion that the mind is *ours,* that it is stable and permanent, a self or an instrument of self. But mind is just mind, a collection of impersonal functions. Its nature is continual change. It isn't you and it isn't I.

CARP: I think we're getting into deep waters here!

BHIKKHU: I hope so. The point I want to make is that when you look at it—*especially* when you look at it—the mind is like a pan of popping popcorn. It just goes on jumping and making a racket and nobody knows what it will do next. It is the best demonstration of impermanence there is. It just keeps changing. No matter how you want it to hold still, it changes. All the aspects of mind are constantly changing: feelings, perceptions, mental formations, and consciousness itself. Wouldn't you agree?

CARP: I guess so. Memories, feelings, all those things keep running on forever.

BHIKKHU: This leads us on to the third mark of existence: non-self, or in Pali, *anattā*.

CARP: I believe I read about that. But it seemed paradoxical to me. I mean, there is no self, but we think there is, only it's just an illusion, and so on.

BHIKKHU: The basic marks of existence aren't obscure in themselves; here again it's our own ignorance, reinforced by craving, that perverts our view. Let's consider non-self in the light of the other two characteristics I've mentioned—unsatisfactoriness and impermanence. Everything in the world is changing, impermanent, not lasting, so it is always, to some degree, liable to suffering or unsatisfactoriness. Anything we like or enjoy we want to *keep on* enjoying, but we can't because it changes, breaks up, drifts away.

CARP: Like my girl friends!

BHIKKHU: We are always liable to be separated from what we love or united with what we hate.

CARP: If you only knew some of the idiots I have to work with.

BHIKKHU: It's unsatisfactory to be where we don't want to be and it's unsatisfactory to lose what we cherish. But that is the unstable nature of things.

CARP: Wait a minute. I thought of something that doesn't cause suffering! My *car*. It's a real beauty, you can see.

BHIKKHU: And it never breaks down?

CARP: Never. Of course, I just bought it two weeks

ago. But it runs perfectly. No problems!

BHIKKHU: Really?

CARP: Sure. Of course, I've got to watch out for it. The other day in the parking lot some idiot opened his door and banged the side! Took out a chip of paint. Unbelievable. Brand new car! I was furious. I could have killed the guy.

BHIKKHU: I see. Was that a pleasant sensation?

CARP (Sheepishly): Actually I felt lousy. It ruined the afternoon. My nerves are pretty bad when I get into conflict. Okay, I know what you'll say. I admit, that was unsatisfactory, that was suffering. The car's paint is impermanent and impermanent things are unsatisfactory.

BHIKKHU: Well, then, amid all this unsatisfactoriness and impermanence, do you see any real self?

CARP: A self? Sure. I see *me*. I see my own self.

BHIKKHU: Be careful now, Mr. Carp. What exactly does this self consist of?

CARP: Well, I'd have to say it's my mind.

BHIKKHU: Buddhism analyzes "mind" into feelings, perceptions, mental formations, and consciousness. Is your self one or all of these?

CARP: Well, I suppose I'd say all.

BHIKKHU: But haven't we established that the mind and its functions are constantly changing?

CARP: Yeah, I guess so.

BHIKKHU: So, if the mind is constantly changing, where is your self from one moment to the next?

CARP: I don't know.

BHIKKHU: Wouldn't it be changing? But in that case what does this self really amount to? What makes it "you" if from moment to moment it changes into something else? When we say "self" we are really talking about some stable identity, aren't we? But where there *is* no stability we can't rightly talk about a self. Furthermore, if the mind is your self, if it is your essence, then why can't you control it at will? Why can't you force it to be calm or happy or creative? And if you can't control it, as you admit, if you can't make it stay here or go there, then *who* does it really belong to? What sort of self is it?

CARP: A pretty poor sort, I must say.

BHIKKHU: Now, this mind, which changes every moment, every instant, which you cannot control at will— does it make you happy? Does it please you?

CARP: Mostly it's a pain, the way my mind runs on.

BHIKKHU: Then if it causes pain, if it's unreliable, if it's constantly in flux, can we honestly call it a self?

CARP: Oh. Wait, now, I'm confused. Perhaps "self" is just a way of speaking.

BHIKKHU: Indeed it is, but what is behind the word? Just a flux of uncontrollable, unreliable conditions.

CARP: Well, Bhikkhu Tissa, I don't know what to say. If you look at it that way, self is a rather flimsy concept.

BHIKKHU: Just so. It's a concept that doesn't accurately reflect the facts. *Events* occur, one after the other, with terrific speed. We can observe the process. But "self" is merely a concept imposed on top of it. When we Buddhists talk about "non-self" or *anattā*, we mean this bare process of events giving rise to other events.

CARP: Yes, I follow your logic, but still I *feel* that I am a self or have a self.

BHIKKHU: On a conventional level, "self" is a perfectly useful term. It's necessary for language and communication. I am I and you are you—that's true enough in everyday language. But the trouble arises when we attribute to self a fundamental reality it doesn't possess. By imagining a precious ego, by believing foolishly that we are permanent and satisfactory "selves," we set ourselves up for suffering.

CARP: Because the universe is *not* permanent or satisfactory?

BHIKKHU: Exactly. Anyone who persists in living contrary to the laws of the universe will continue to experience suffering.

CARP: This is really extraordinary. I'm going to have to think this over. But you haven't convinced me, not at all!

BHIKKHU: These three marks of existence—impermanence, unsatisfactoriness, and non-self—are significant because they indicate the way the universe *is*, and the sort of conditions we have to deal with. Unfortunately, most of us, out of ignorance, see things incorrectly. We take what is changing as stable; we take what is imperfect and unsatisfactory as satisfactory; we take what is without a self as having a self.

CARP: If what you say is true, then most people are living exactly backwards to the way they should be living.

BHIKKHU: Yes, and that in itself is another aspect of *dukkha* or unsatisfactoriness.

CARP: All right, you Buddhists do have some justification for talking about suffering. But one thing I still don't understand is *why* people misinterpret the world so grossly. Is it simply out of ignorance?

BHIKKHU: When we talk about ignorance we mean more than the absence of information. We mean self-deception and lack of judgment as well. For example, if we have a problem to solve, we can gather information about the problem and from that information come to a conclusion. But what if the information is faulty? What if we have misunderstood the facts to start with? Then we begin reasoning with false premises, and no matter how clever we are our conclusions will turn out false, too. The problem of understanding life itself depends on properly understanding facts. When we are ignorant and uninstructed we tend to take things at face value. Human nature being what it is, we gravitate toward pleasant objects and shun unpleasant objects. Because we are fond of pleasure, we try to magnify it wherever we see it, and because we hate pain we magnify that. Simply speaking, we run to extremes. We have no special motivation to analyze the objects of our senses as long as they keep us entertained, as they do so well. Moreover, because we live a fair number of years and because there is a continuity in our experience, we fasten onto the notion that we are selves or souls who experience things and have a definite identity. We don't know any better, and without investigation we have no particular reason to question this life of loves and hates and quick assumptions. We rely on our ignorant biases and continue to suffer.

CARP: This ignorance sounds like plain carelessness and stupidity.

BHIKKHU: Yes. To the Buddha, ignorance is not just a neutral not-knowing; it is a very reprehensible defilement, a dangerous and foolish self-deception.

CARP: Now *there's* a funny old word. "Defilement." It sounds so negative. Who would want to believe in "defilement" nowadays?

BHIKKHU: Well, I ask you, who would want to escape suffering?

CARP: There is a connection?

BHIKKHU: Of course. Ignorance is the basic defilement, the source of all greed, hatred, and delusion. A mind clouded by defilements cannot see reality. Not understanding, not seeing the marks of impermanence, suffering, and non-self, a person acts as if things were quite the contrary. Thus arises conflict with the laws of nature, and misery follows.

CARP: But how exactly does this misery come about?

BHIKKHU: Are you familiar with the Four Noble Truths?

CARP: Oh, them. Yes, I read about them. They sounded depressing at the time.

BHIKKHU: But not now?

CARP: Well, I'm thinking about it.

BHIKKHU: Sometimes people only hear the first noble truth, which states the universal problem—that life passes away, that it breaks up, that health gives way to sickness and life gives way to death, that all experiences and components of ordinary existence are impermanent and flawed. Not that they are necessarily suffering all the time—indeed, they are sometimes full of pleasure—but they are always liable to suffering.

CARP: That is a pretty sobering assessment.

BHIKKHU: The second noble truth is the origin of suffering. Suffering has a cause. This is a deceptively simple statement that contains much meaning. Suffering does not happen spontaneously. It is caused and conditioned by other phenomena. As the primary cause, the Buddha singled out craving. Wherever this craving or obsessive desire springs up, suffering is sure to follow. Why? Because craving leads to grasping and clinging to what is inherently unstable. All delightful objects, experiences, and persons break up and disappear, so when ever we indulge in craving we are bound for disappointment and pain.

CARP: All right, I am with you so far. But how do we get out of this mess?

BHIKKHU: The first two noble truths state the problem. The second two reveal the solution. The third noble truth is called the truth of the cessation or ending of suffering.

CARP: Well, it's about time!

BHIKKHU: The Buddha realized that every phenomenon that arises, arises from causes and conditions, and that when those causes and conditions are removed, the phenomenon must disappear. Suffering has a cause. The cause is craving. When craving is brought to an end, suffering is also brought to an end.

CARP: But that's easier said than done, I expect.

BHIKKHU: Yes, and that's where the fourth noble truth comes in. The Buddha states that there is a problem, namely suffering; there is a cause of the problem; there is the possibility of eliminating the problem; and finally there is a specific way to eliminate the problem. The fourth noble truth is simply the Noble Eightfold Path, the Buddha's prescription for dealing with the unsatisfactoriness in life. The eight factors of the path are eight virtues or skills which can gradually weaken and ultimately destroy the craving that oppresses us. Right Views means having a correct understanding of the way the universe operates, the way suffering springs up in our lives. Right Intentions means directing our thoughts and intentions toward wholesome things, toward kindness, mental purity, and self-training. Right Speech means refraining from harsh, false, or useless speech. Right Action means acting in a virtuous way, carrying out our intentions, and following the moral precepts. Right Livelihood means earning a living by honest and respectable means, fairly, not cheating anyone, not harming any living creatures. Right Effort means making an effort to guard the mind, to overcome unwholesome mental states such as greed and hatred and to replace them with generosity and loving-kindness. Right Mindfulness means developing attention and presence of mind, not being careless or unobservant. Right Concentration means focusing the mind skillfully on objects so as to know them deeply without being distracted. These eight factors summarize the training.

CARP: I hate to criticize, Bhikkhu Tissa, but that word "training" has an unpleasant sound. Life's hard enough. Who wants any more "training" than he has to endure already?

BHIKKHU: What makes you think this training is disagreeable?

CARP: I mean, all those factors, all that discipline. I don't think I'd like to take it all on me.

BHIKKHU: Pardon me, but the purpose is to take it all *off* you.

CARP: I don't understand.

BHIKKHU: Buddhism as a religion—or as a way of life—aims at *lightening* your burden, not increasing it. It is the untrained, undisciplined mind that is weighed down and obstructed with woe, just as a person who has no training in finding his way in a jungle is likely to lose the path and struggle miserably through thick vines and thorns. We are so accustomed to carrying unpleasant burdens that we can only think of taking on new, *pleasant* burdens, instead of putting them *all* down. The Dhamma is a training in putting down. As such, it liberates and gladdens us.

CARP: Well, now, Bhikkhu Tissa, I've got to say I *enjoy* some of these "burdens." Why should I get rid of them when they are really the only things that make my life worthwhile?

BHIKKHU: Here we have arrived at an important point, Mr. Carp. Every person has pleasant, unpleasant, and neutral experiences. Naturally we prefer the pleasant. But the burdens I refer to are not the experiences themselves. They are our *attachments* to those experiences.

CARP: Ah, you're getting subtle on me.

BHIKKHU: Remember, the Buddha identifies craving as the primary cause of our pain, disappointment, and suffering. This craving or mental hunger is a strain or burden on the mind. It causes us to struggle against the natural, changing state of things. For instance, suppose we hunger after some desirable object and try to obtain it. Then we suffer the strain of longing, the worry about getting the object, the fear that somebody else will get it first, and the uncertainty of whether we really have the means to obtain it. If we fail to achieve our ends, our inflamed mind suffers disappointment. If we do get what we want, then we have to protect it, take care of it, see that it is not stolen or destroyed. So we suffer anxiety on account of our craving and attachment. Then we have to deal with the unfaithfulness of our own mind. The mind changes! We may decide we don't like the object after all, so we have the worry of getting rid of it. Or the object turns out to cause us problems of one kind or another. Then our attachment turns to aversion and we suffer the misery of being united with what we don't like. Or suppose we continue to enjoy the object. Not only does the mind change, the *object* changes. It breaks, it runs away, it rusts, it gets old. Sooner or later we are separated from it, and then we feel grief. Then, not knowing any better, to cover up this grief, our insatiable mind goes lurching after some *new* object, mental or material. And the wheel keeps turning through the seconds and through the years. And we do not escape.

CARP: Bhikkhu Tissa, there's a lot of truth in what you say. I can't deny it. But how *else* can a person live, if not by reaching for things? How can anyone be happy?

BHIKKHU: Indeed, we must reach for things, but the *right* things and in the right way. To put down the burden of craving does not mean to stop acting in the world. It means to cut off our foolish hunger and vanity. The virtuous man, the happy man, is one who follows the middle way, who is moderate in his desires. Buddhism teaches that good results follow good actions and evil results follow evil actions. Events cause and condition other events, so we should act responsibly, knowing that we do, in effect, shape our own future. When we cut off an impulse of blind craving we gain peace in this very moment because the mind is no longer irritated, and we gain benefit in the future because we have set up no painful cycle of grasping and losing. It is advantageous to live simply without superfluous possessions and entanglements, but the most important thing is to root out craving itself.

CARP: So I don't necessarily have to give up things?

BHIKKHU: Ah, Mr. Carp, you must give up what is painful. You must give up what hurts.

CARP: And craving hurts?

BHIKKHU: Just look at your own mind, that's all.

CARP: Do you think I should meditate?

BHIKKHU: I think you should examine yourself and watch the changes in your mind and body.

CARP: Where does all this lead, Bhikkhu Tissa? Does it lead to happiness?

BHIKKHU: Yes, but not happiness as most people have been conditioned to think. True happiness is not the piling up of sense-pleasures. True happiness comes from liberation from the defilements, from clear sight, from an open, generous heart that does not fear the ceaseless change of things.

CARP: What about all this I've read about "supramundane wisdom"?

BHIKKHU: Wisdom arises from the practice of Dhamma. It is a tool that helps us reach the goal, but it is not the goal itself.

CARP: The goal is the end of suffering, right?

BHIKKHU: Right. Some people develop what you might call a craving after wisdom—wanting to know the secrets of the workings of things, out of curiosity or pride. This is knowing for its own sake, and it is not useful. In fact, the Buddha refused to answer speculative questions about the origin and the future of the universe, because such questions are distractions from the matter at hand—the problem of suffering and the overcoming of suffering.

CARP: You know, I had the idea that Buddhism was only concerned with very lofty, esoteric things—not the everyday existence of ordinary people. It's somewhat encouraging to hear that Buddhism deals with how to achieve happiness in this world. Not that I necessarily *believe* it, of course.

BHIKKHU: Sometimes people who are too much caught up in the world turn cynical, thinking that there is nothing higher than the gaining and losing of status, objects, or relationships. Not seeing that a higher, worthier, and more peaceful everyday life is possible, they become bogged down in entertainments that fail to satisfy.

CARP: I wonder if you're referring to me, Bhikkhu Tissa. Well, it doesn't matter. I can testify that lots of my unreligious friends just don't believe that any different kind of life exists. You're suggesting that it does.

BHIKKHU: The Dhamma suggests that it does. Now let me return to your charge of pessimism.

CARP: Well, I'm having second thoughts about that.

BHIKKHU: Buddhism deals with the problem of suffering and the cure of suffering. Once we recognize that a disease exists we can treat the disease if we have the medicine at hand. Imagine the joy of health to someone who has never before known health. Imagine the relief of someone who has carried a boulder on his back all his life and now can set it down.

CARP: Yes, I can see that. But really, Bhikkhu Tissa, I don't want to go live in a cave and meditate all the time. I've got to make a living in this world.

BHIKKHU: There's no need to live in a cave. The practice of Dhamma can and should be carried on wherever you find yourself. It is compatible with any kind of respectable livelihood. It depends on mindfully observing our actions from moment to moment, whatever we are doing, and so it can benefit the businessman as well as the monk.

CARP: Well, my friend Charlie Prentice sure seems cheerful lately. But a fellow has got to figure out what is best for *him*. Tell me, if I wanted to—if a person wanted to practise Buddhism, to follow the Dhamma, what should he do? I'm speaking hypothetically, of course. How does somebody become a Buddhist?

BHIKKHU: Somebody becomes a Buddhist by following the teachings of the Buddha.

CARP: Like the Noble Eightfold Path?

BHIKKHU: Yes. But there's a brief saying that covers it all: to abstain from all evil, to cultivate the good, and to purify the mind—this is the teaching of all the Buddhas.

CARP: That sounds pretty good. Could you explain just a bit?

BHIKKHU: To abstain from all evil means to refrain from all actions that cause harm to oneself or others. It means to follow the Five Precepts: to avoid killing, stealing, sexual misconduct, lying, and taking intoxicants.

CARP: I'm afraid I've been known to break a few of those precepts! Do you mean, for instance, that I shouldn't kill at all? Like not stepping on these ants crawling all around here?

BHIKKHU: The precepts protect not only all animals; they protect you as well, because they keep you from doing actions which will coarsen your mind and cause you suffering later on.

CARP: But suppose somebody just can't keep all these precepts perfectly?

BHIKKHU: The precepts are not commandments. The Buddha wasn't a god who laid down absolute rules. The Buddha did, however, perfectly understand the world, and he simply pointed out that when someone keeps the precepts he is acting according to Dhamma and building up protection and happiness for himself and other beings. The closer we can live to the precepts the better it is for us.

CARP: Keeping those precepts would certainly make you think. Now, how about doing good?

BHIKKHU: Avoiding evil is the first step. But beyond that we have to act virtuously and generously. A Buddhist is expected to demonstrate his kindness by helping his fellow beings, by making an effort to have a positive effect on his society. He should show the blessings of the Dhamma in his own conduct.

CARP: And what about purifying the mind?

BHIKKHU: The practitioner restrains his unwholesome impulses by observing the precepts and he becomes a force for good through his own will. And through it all he should strive to cleanse himself of the defilements of greed, hatred, and delusion, and the ignorance that spawns them. He should move steadily, at whatever pace is suitable for him, toward deliverance from all suffering, toward enlightenment.

CARP: What you describe is impressive, really. How can an ordinary guy do such a thing? I'm not really a strong person, I know. I am what I am mainly out of weakness, I guess.

BHIKKHU: Mr. Carp, let me emphasize one thing especially. The Dhamma is the noble path for *everyone*, weak or strong or in between. Do what you can, because every act of kindness or virtue or mindfulness takes you a step closer to deliverance from sorrow.

CARP: You're really serious about this, aren't you? I wish I could be like that—serious, confident. You know, the trouble is, I'm so restless, I can't sit still. So I go racing here and there all the time. My mind wanders, so *I* wander too.

BHIKKHU: This wandering is called *saṁsāra*, the cycle of birth and death.

CARP: That's depressing.

BHIKKHU: Indeed it is. And that's why the Dhamma is such a relief. It can free us from that cycle.

CARP: We're all wanderers in a way, aren't we?

BHIKKHU: Yes. You and I and—and even that big red ant crawling up your leg.

CARP: *Yeow!*

(Mr. Carp jumps up and dances around wildly, brushing at his pants.)

CARP: Ow! Get off! Get off! These things will bite!

BHIKKHU: Easy now, Mr. Carp. It dropped off.

CARP: It did?

BHIKKHU: It probably considered you an unsteady surface.

CARP (Laughing suddenly): I am! I am an unsteady surface!

(Bhikkhu Tissa stands up, smiling.)

BHIKKHU: And what will you do about that?

CARP (Embarrassed): Well, I don't know. Say, listen, I've taken up enough of your time. Thanks for explaining things. I'd better get going. I'm heading down to the beach to meet some friends.

BHIKKHU: I hope you have a safe drive.

CARP: Oh, I will, I will. It's a great car, a beauty, you can see. Oh no! No! Did you see that *bird?* Did you see what that bird just *did* to my car?

BHIKKHU: Yes, birds will do that.

CARP (Shaking his head): I just had it waxed! You know, that makes me think—oh, never mind. Thanks for your time, Bhikkhu Tissa.

(Smiling to himself, Bhikkhu Tissa takes his broom in hand again.)

BHIKKHU: I'm glad you dropped by, Mr. Carp.

CARP: Yeah, me too, I guess.

Bhikkhu Tissa Meets a Skeptic

BHIKKHU: If you'll excuse me, I'll get back to my work now.

CARP (Hesitantly): Oh sure, sure. Say, you know, if you need any help around the temple, I wouldn't mind lending a hand sometime.

BHIKKHU: That's kind of you, but we manage pretty well.

CARP: No, I'm serious, I'd be glad to help, anytime. Really!

BHIKKHU: Well then, would you like to sweep? The sidewalk out there needs it.

CARP (Startled): You mean now? But you've only got one broom.

BHIKKHU: Oh, there's another one in the toolshed there.

Bhikkhu Tissa turns away and placidly resumes his sweeping. Mr. Carp fidgets for a moment, then goes and gets the other broom from the shed. He returns and waits awkwardly for instructions, but gets none. Finally he begins sweeping the sidewalk, casting puzzled looks at the monk. At one point he opens his mouth to say something, but shuts it again. Bhikkhu Tissa is no longer paying attention to him. With a bemused expression, Mr. Carp applies himself to sweeping the sidewalk. Little puffs of dust and leaves fly out to either side as the broom finds its rhythm. A morning breeze has now sprung up, swaying the trees above and sending flickers of light and dark, sun and shade, across the sweepers.

BHIKKHU TISSA
AND THE GREATER GOOD

It is noon on a winter day. Bhikkhu Tissa has been a guest for a mid-day meal in the home of a married couple, Leona and Ernest, and now sits with them in the family room, sipping a cup of tea. The windows of the room look out on a snowy landscape. A fire leaps and crackles in the fireplace.

LEONA: Was everything all right, Bhikkhu Tissa?

BHIKKHU TISSA: Just fine, thank you.

LEONA: Of course, you know I'm referring to the food, not the state of the universe!

BHIKKHU: Yes, I thought as much. It was delicious.

LEONA: The universe is quite another question, right?

ERNEST: I've got to apologize for my wife, venerable sir. She never stops philosophizing!

LEONA: Ernest, my dear husband, I am a woman made for grand ideas!

ERNEST: How well I know. Are you going to bombard this venerable monk with impossible questions?

LEONA (Laughing): Oh, I think he can take care of himself. Anyway, Ernest, you were the one who invited him. You must have something on that oh-so-serious mind of yours.

ERNEST: Well, I did think it might be useful to have a private little discussion about matters of substance.

LEONA: Do you hear that, Venerable? My husband talks like an office memo. Why then do I love him?

BHIKKHU (Smiling over his teacup): Wise men refrain from trying to figure out love.

ERNEST: As you know, I've been getting interested in Buddhism over the last year, and sometimes it seems like it raises more questions than it answers!

BHIKKHU: Oh yes, that often happens at first. I think it's a good sign. If Buddhism is to have a real effect on somebody it must challenge them, make them think of a hundred problems and puzzles they never considered before. The average person all too often takes things for granted, has a careless, habitual way of looking at the world, and idly believes in unexamined concepts. But Buddhism kicks the props entirely out from under such habits and reveals many unanswered questions which have been there all along.

LEONA: Are you referring to big stuff like the meaning of life, and so on?

BHIKKHU: No, just basic laws and relationships that we need to grasp little by little until we can tackle the bigger questions. Sometimes simple intellectual curiosity can start this process. Sometimes it's a single provocative incident.

ERNEST: That's sort of what happened to me—an incident. I've been studying Buddhism for a while, maybe with a little more interest than Leona here ...

LEONA: There he goes, bragging already.

ERNEST: . . . and then just recently a question arose that has no end of implications. It has to do with a job offer.

LEONA: Oh, you're going into this, are you? Venerable Tissa, we've talked this over fifty times and I think he's crazy—dear, but crazy. Well, Ernest, tell our guest. Maybe he'll straighten you out.

ERNEST: My field is chemistry, Bhikkhu Tissa, and I've been in and out of academia and private industry over the years. At the moment I've got a teaching position at the college that I like pretty well, though it doesn't pay a lot. Recently I got a very attractive job offer from the research division of a local chemical company. It would mean a sizable increase in salary and a chance to do some creative work in my particular specialty. Professionally it would be a big step up for me, and, as a matter of fact, I know some of the people there and I think we'd get along fine. But I can't make up my mind to take the job. And it's all because of something you said.

BHIKKHU: What was that?

ERNEST: You were talking about the Noble Eightfold Path and you mentioned Right Livelihood. You said one should earn a living without harming others. Now, does this apply to animals?

BHIKKHU: Yes, it does.

ERNEST: I thought so. There's the problem. You see, this company has a research laboratory where they test the effects of their chemicals on animals. I wouldn't be directly connected with that department, I wouldn't do any experiments on animals, but still I'd feel uncomfortably close. And that bothers me.

BHIKKHU: What do they do to the animals there?

ERNEST: Toxicity tests, mostly. That means they poison them—dogs, cats, rabbits, rats, and other animals. They paint chemicals into the eyes of rabbits and see what concentrations will cause ulcers and blindness. They force-feed lethal compounds to groups of dogs and see how long it takes for half of them to die.

BHIKKHU: What happens to the other half?

ERNEST: They might use them again in other tests. More often they kill them all. They "sacrifice" them, to use the euphemism. Sometimes they do autopsies.

LEONA: Earnest, please, you're making me ill.

ERNEST: I got a brief look at the lab when they were giving me a tour of the company. Now, I've known about such labs all my professional life, but I've never worked in one or really paid too much attention. But after studying Buddhism a little, I found that it really upset me to see the animals in cages and the instruments and so on. The guy who was giving me the tour must have noticed because he said, "Don't worry, your office is far away, you won't hear anything." "They make *noise*?" I said. And he said, "Oh, not so much" and sort of shrugged. Since then I literally haven't been able to sleep. I keep imagining sitting in my office in another part of the building and hearing faint screams coming up through the ventilation ducts or something.

LEONA: This is how he's been going on, Bhikkhu Tissa. I tell him *he* doesn't have to have anything to do with animal experiments, so why worry about it?

ERNEST: Thinking about the suffering of animals, Bhikkhu Tissa, I find my mind wandering out in wider and wider circles, trying to make sense of a world that seems, well, pretty horrible in many respects. But to begin with, I'd just like to have your opinion about whether or not I should take this job.

BHIKKHU: I wonder if you would really be satisfied if I said, yes, you should, or no, you shouldn't. Sometimes Buddhist teaching has a specific answer to a moral question, sometimes not. In either case what is important is that the student understand the underlying principles himself so that he doesn't just rely on faith in the teacher. You began your reflections with Right Livelihood, so let's pick up there. Right Livelihood means earning a living in a harmless, honest, and inoffensive manner. The Buddha advised his disciples specifically to refrain from dealing in arms, in living beings, in meat, in intoxicants, and in poisons.

LEONA: You know, that covers a whole lot of occupations, venerable sir! I mean—making guns, bombs, all kinds of weapons. And as for living beings and meat, well, you are talking about huge industries there. And do you mean to say that dealing in *all* kinds of intoxicants is prohibited—beer, wine, and everything? And you could include a host of products under the name of "poisons," everything from nerve gas to bug spray. Do you really believe that everybody working in all of these industries is necessarily evil? Are they all going to suffer some terrible karma? Are they going to hell?

ERNEST: Hold on, Leona, give Bhikkhu Tissa a chance to answer.

BHIKKHU: The Buddha teaches that for our own well-being and the well-being of others we should avoid these classes of occupations. Dealing in arms means just what you think—all kinds of weapons and instruments for killing. Dealing in living beings refers to animals, of course, and it also extends into areas like slavery, or prostitution, or the buying and selling of children or adults in one way or another. "Meat" refers to the bodies of beings after they are killed. And poisons are just as you say—all kinds of toxic products designed to kill.

LEONA: Those are immense categories.

BHIKKHU: The categories are wide because the principle is wide: not to engage in occupations which cause suffering, destruction, and death. Now, you ask whether somebody who works in one of these occupations necessarily suffers misfortune as a result.

LEONA: Yes, what about the perfectly honest owner of a liquor store? Or a sporting goods dealer who sells guns to hunters?

BHIKKHU: *Kamma,* or karma, means volitional actions by body, speech, or mind. Kamma produces a result for the doer according to its nature as wholesome, unwholesome, or neutral. Acts of killing and harming, for instance, will sooner or later bring painful results for the doer.

LEONA: Yes, I understand that. That's the practical basis for Buddhist moral precepts. But if one *doesn't* actually kill or harm or steal, and so on, then it seems that one could be engaged in almost any profession.

BHIKKHU: To sell liquor or guns, assuming one does so honestly, may not in itself bring karmic misfortune. But with the factor of Right Livelihood the Buddha recognizes the truth that habitual associations strongly influence our thoughts and deeds. There may be someone, for instance, who works in a slaughterhouse, but whose job is not to kill animals but only to grade meat or operate a conveyor belt. He may not actually break the precepts or do evil, but this is nevertheless wrong livelihood because his mind is likely to be harmed by the unwholesome atmosphere. He becomes accustomed to pain and death. He regards the suffering of living beings as unimportant. And thus he sinks further into ignorance and becomes easier prey for mental defilements which will definitely cause him sorrow. The principle is the same for intoxicants or weapons. Dealing with these, a person becomes indifferent to the delusion and destruction that alcohol and drugs cause, or becomes callous about the killing or maiming of living beings by weapons.

LEONA: But these are popular goods and services. There will always be *somebody* to provide them.

BHIKKHU: True, Leona, but it needn't be *you*.

LEONA: Oh, dear, I can see what you think about Ernest's job offer!

Bhikkhu Tissa and the Greater Good

BHIKKHU: Maybe you are guessing a little too quickly. Let's analyze the question further. Yes, to do painful experiments on animals in one's work, to wound, poison, or torment them in any way, is certainly a violation of Right Livelihood.

ERNEST: You would condemn such an occupation, then?

BHIKKHU: Yes. To inflict pain on living beings—even for the supposed advantage of other living beings—is cruel and short-sighted.

ERNEST: Ah, well!

BHIKKHU: But I would not exactly on that account advise you to reject your job offer.

ERNEST: I don't understand.

BHIKKHU: I believe you said your job would *not* involve experimenting on animals, and you would not be directly connected with it.

ERNEST: Strictly speaking, no.

BHIKKHU: Then strictly speaking you would not be violating the principle of Right Livelihood. According to Buddhism we are karmically responsible only for what we do intentionally and what we order others to do. Beyond that, it's up to the individual to decide. Right Livelihood is a flexible concept that can guide us regarding professions that were unknown in the Buddha's time. We have to decide how close we can come to occupations that are definitely unwholesome without becoming contaminated. Ultimately, almost every profession is somehow related to every other, so we would likely go crazy if we looked for a job that was not distantly, theoretically, harmful to somebody. Take a big company with many divisions or subsidiaries. Is somebody in one department responsible for what somebody in another department does? Is the typist in New York implicated in the killing of cattle in Texas?

ERNEST: No, that's unreasonable, in my opinion.

BHIKKHU: So, it comes down to this: you must be quite sure and satisfied in your own mind that you are not willingly doing any harmful deeds and that you are not encouraging or condoning the ill-treatment of living beings.

ERNEST: Oh, that's so hard to know . . .

LEONA: Well and good, Venerable Tissa. But don't we have to balance off harm and benefit? I'm not willing to concede that doing scientific experiments on animals is entirely evil. Think of the lasting benefits to humanity that come of such experiments.

ERNEST: Uh, Leona, at this lab they're presently testing oven-cleaner and hair-spray.

LEONA: Oh. Not the most vital products, I grant you.

ERNEST: And before you go on to cite penicillin or some other wonder drug, I think it's fair to note that medicines can be developed and tested without recourse to live animal subjects. We now have sophisticated techniques of computer-modeling and tissue-culture that are accurate and cause no bloodshed. The fact that animals have been used so much in the past does not prove that discoveries would have been im-

Bhikkhu Tissa and the Greater Good   41

possible *without* them, only that that has been the habit, or conditioned reflex, of scientific researchers.

LEONA: Maybe, maybe. But, Bhikkhu Tissa, I want to get at the philosophical question here. If some real benefit to humanity can come about through experimenting on animals, even though they suffer, then why not use them? Shouldn't we be concerned with the greater good that will result?

BHIKKHU: I'm glad you raise the question of benefit, Leona, because this is where people often go astray when considering Right Livelihood or those troublesome five precepts. Yes, I agree that we should act for the greater good, but—and here is a question that has sent seekers into the Sangha for centuries—how do we know what the greater good *is?*

LEONA: It's whatever benefits the most people, I guess.

BHIKKHU: Only people? What about animals?

LEONA: Well, people are more important.

BHIKKHU: Indeed? To whom?

LEONA: To people. Okay, I know it sounds self-serving.

BHIKKHU: Leaving animals out for the moment, suppose some action helps us but harms other people. How do you evaluate it? Where is the greater good?

LEONA: I guess you just have to choose.

BHIKKHU: On what basis?

LEONA: Oh, Bhikkhu Tissa, I can see you won't be satisfied with anything less than a moral foundation—a religious foundation!

BHIKKHU: Better to say, a foundation on reality. And the question remains: How do we know the greater good?

ERNEST: Through study of the Dhamma, I would guess.

BHIKKHU: Through study and *practice* of the Dhamma. The Buddha teaches that we should do certain things and avoid other things, but not on his word alone or the words of our teachers or out of respect for tradition. We are told to test these teachings in our own minds and in our own practice and then put our faith in the Dhamma as we see its effects.

LEONA: Yes, I will say that is one of the attractive qualities of Buddhism.

BHIKKHU: Let me ask you, what do you think is the ultimate goal of Buddhism?

LEONA: I know that: to put an end to suffering. But we can't really call that the greater good, can we? We need something more specific.

BHIKKHU: The end of suffering, or *Nibbāna*, is what the entire Dhamma points to. The Buddha said that just as the great ocean has only one taste, the taste of salt, so the Dhamma has only one taste, the taste of liberation. In the Buddhist view, every specific goal—to use your word—must be connected to the ultimate goal to be worthwhile. We have been discussing Right Livelihood. Now, Right Livelihood is not the ultimate goal but in a sense it recapitulates the whole. We want to escape the suffering involved with making a living—the disagreements, difficulties, guilt, anxiety, and so on. To accomplish this we first of all have to place ourselves in conditions where such unpleasantness is least likely to arise; that is, in those occupations which are peaceful, non-threatening, undisturbing to the conscience, and compatible with high ideals. Second, we see to it that we conduct our business or perform our job in a scrupulously fair and honest manner. This frees us from the suffering inherent in trickery and cheating. It helps us get along with our co-workers and the public at large and gives us the security of a good reputation. Finally, by getting our livelihood with energy and effort in a lawful, honest, and harmless manner, we liberate ourselves from self-contempt and the disgust of base money-grubbing, so that one large area of our lives is protected from the worst danger—the danger of our own misguided action. Thus we enjoy the satisfaction of honourable work. This is purification of the mind with regard to livelihood.

ERNEST: It seems that the Buddha overlooked nothing that might contribute to happiness. But still, even if we behave in the manner you suggest, we can't be sure that making a living is going to be free of problems.

LEONA: Yes, *everybody*—good, evil, and average—complains about his or her job. Even in the most blameless work there's some suffering.

BHIKKHU: Very true. Right Livelihood has a beneficial ripple-effect we cannot see the end of, but certainly it will not eradicate *all* suffering. There are, if you remember, seven more factors of the Noble Eightfold Path to develop.

LEONA (Laughing): Ah, I might have known! This Buddhism is nothing if not methodical! There's a sort of—well, a sort of beauty about the way it fits together—like an exquisite watch.

ERNEST: Or like the molecular structure of DNA! (All three laugh.)

LEONA: This business of getting through life is certainly complicated. We started with rabbits in cages and now where are we?

ERNEST: One eighth of the way to enlightenment?

LEONA: Oh you! But let's get an answer from the venerable monk. Okay, I see the need for Right Livelihood in a practical sense, but why do we need to link it with anything else? Why buy the whole deal, so to speak?

BHIKKHU: I think, Leona, that you've forgotten what you just said. You noted that even a perfectly blameless livelihood will not remove *all* suffering. Now, how much more suffering is there in life?

LEONA: Oh, heaps and heaps!

BHIKKHU: Are you willing to endure it? Are you ready for it?

LEONA: No, not at all, no, categorically no.

BHIKKHU: Do you think you can escape it simply by wishing to? Do you think that suffering—disease, old age, loss, grief, and so on—will just pass you by?

LEONA (Sighing): No, I don't think that.

BHIKKHU: Well, do you believe *you* have any

power in the matter?

LEONA: Maybe. I don't know. I'm not sure.

BHIKKHU: Buddhism teaches that we do have power to reduce and ultimately eliminate suffering. When somebody makes even a small effort to follow the basic precepts he reaps an immediate benefit in the form of a pacified mind. Good qualities—peace-bringing qualities—are strengthened and bad qualities are ever so slightly weakened. When somebody makes a really systematic and conscientious effort to avoid killing, stealing, lying, sexual misconduct, and taking intoxicants, he fortifies himself further. When he pursues the good by acting out of benevolence and compassion he stores up benefit for the future. Then when he tries to purify his *mind* as well as his deeds he is moving positively to the greater good—Nibbāna, deliverance, the end of sorrow.

ERNEST: I don't doubt what you say, venerable sir, but with all due respect, we are lay people living very much in the world, with many responsibilities and burdens. How can we realistically concern ourselves with getting to Nibbāna?

BHIKKHU: Nibbāna isn't a place to get to. It's not even a state of mind. The Buddha called it simply the end of suffering. This is a goal that should concern everybody regardless of his or her worldly station. The Noble Eightfold Path is a transcendent way that leads out of the world to the inconceivable bliss of Nibbana, but it is also consistent with an active life *in* the world along the way. I mean by this that the

Dhamma protects us now, in our daily problems and challenges, and later, in the kind of future our deeds will lead us to. Some people, when they hear the transcendent promise of the Dhamma, are elated. Others, like you, perhaps, are a little worried, thinking that they are not ready to ascend any spiritual summits. Really, there is no cause for worry. If we apply ourselves to solving immediate problems as the Buddha teaches, then higher goals will simply come into focus in their own time. We need only remind ourselves that there lies ahead of us a greater good which is timeless, steady, and ultimately accessible. Simple moral restraint and deeds of charity and the practice of mindfulness in the household life cannot fail to build a foundation for wisdom.

ERNEST: I have an instinct that what you say is true. That's why I'm trying to order my life at least to the extent of giving wisdom a *chance* to arise. But I'm not sure. Life is often mysterious, like a wandering in the dark.

BHIKKHU: You are right. Life is very mysterious. But in the Buddhist system even that mystery is a suitable theme for meditation. For instance, look out the window here. From where we sit we can't see the ground, only that blank gray sky and a few snowflakes drifting past. If we didn't know better we might think those snowflakes just appear spontaneously in our field of view and whirl out of it again into some kind of oblivion, without a reason, uncaused, absurdly appearing and disappearing.

LEONA: That would be just delusion, just ignorance.

BHIKKHU: But because we have some experience, because we have at one time or another stuck our heads out the window, we know that snow falls from the clouds overhead and it piles up in drifts on the ground beneath. We see where it comes from and where it goes. It's the same with the larger questions of life: investigation destroys ignorance. Somebody might keep moral precepts just out of fear, or tradition, or habit—and there's nothing really wrong with this, it's still a help and protection. But sooner or later most people think, "Why am I really following these rules? Where will they lead me?" If a monk or somebody tells them the purpose is to get rid of suffering, then, if they're intelligent, they want to find out for themselves how and why.

LEONA: Exactly, exactly.

BHIKKHU: The Buddha discovered and made known the path to deliverance. Now, it's a sorry old world we live in, but that path is still open, friends, it is still open.

ERNEST: Perhaps Leona and I are following it already, even without being fully aware. But I would hate to think, Bhikkhu Tissa, that all the mystery must go out of life.

BHIKKHU: Ignorance must go, but mystery in the sense I think you mean comes even more alive in the objects of our experience. Our wonder at the infinite and ineffable is an intuition of Nibbāna itself. Looking here through this plain glass window on emptiness—even though we have no illusions about where those snowflakes come from and where they go, still we find it peaceful and uplifting to gaze out on those random crystals.

ERNEST: Yes, that's true. But why should that be?

(Bhikkhu Tissa smiles, says nothing, gazes thoughtfully out the window.)

LEONA: Perhaps because—if I might be so bold—because looking out in that dimensionless space we are reminded of our connections to infinite things. I mean, the flake that bumps against our windowpane here is connected to the clouds and the clouds to the whole atmosphere and the atmosphere to the space beyond, with its matter and energy and vast laws of generation and destruction. One can't help feeling part of a cosmic drama, so to speak.

ERNEST: Ah, what a philosopher you are, Leona!

LEONA: And what of it? I think Venerable Tissa would approve. That's what Buddhism teaches, isn't it? Investigation?

BHIKKHU: Yes, and when we investigate we see connections, and when we see connections we are motivated to act in certain ways.

ERNEST: But why act at all? Isn't passive contemplation enough?

BHIKKHU: No. The mindful observation of the world that the Buddha recommends reveals that intentional deeds have results for the doer. We are where we are—in fortune or misfortune, peace or

Bhikkhu Tissa and the Greater Good 49

trouble—as a result of what we have done in the past. Where we go in the future depends on what we do now.

LEONA: Are you talking about rebirth? Well, that seems to me like a rather weak motivation, since rebirth is not at all apparent to me. It may very well be true, but I mean to say that I just don't see it in front of me as a reality the same way I see other facts about mind and matter that Buddhism talks about. I've read that sutta you referred to where the Buddha says we shouldn't accept any teaching until we see for ourselves that it is true.

BHIKKHU: I see you remember the first part of the *Kālāma Sutta*, but do you remember the second part?

LEONA: The second?

BHIKKHU: After giving specific examples of wrong reasons for believing a teaching, the Buddha goes on to lead the skeptical Kālāmas into the Dhamma. He asks them whether greed, hate, and delusion are wholesome or unwholesome and whether they lead to suffering or not. The Kālāmas make the obvious answer that they are unwholesome and lead to suffering. In response to further questions they agree that the absence of these defilements and the positive cultivation of morality lead to blessing and happiness in this life. If this is so, the Buddha goes on to say, then there are four consolations for whomever is devoted to virtue. First, if there is a future world and if good and bad deeds have results for the doer, then the virtuous person knows himself safe and can expect a happy situation. Second, if there is no rebirth and if deeds have no future effect, then he at least lives happily in this world, without worry. Third, if evil things happen to evildoers, then he, who does no evil, is secure and free from harm. Fourth, if no evil things happen to evildoers, then he in any event will not meet with evil fortune.

LEONA: That's well said. Even a hardened skeptic would have to admire that reasoning. And if one goes *that* far one would have to admit that it would be wise to pay more attention to one's behaviour and even set out on a more systematic path of spiritual practice.

ERNEST: Such as the Noble Eightfold Path, Leona?

LEONA (Laughing): Why yes, now that you mention it. We keep coming back to that, don't we?

BHIKKHU (Smiling): Well, we *should* come back to it. But I hope you understand that this path is a path of practice and self-development and mindful investigation. It's not necessary at the outset to believe in rebirth or other difficult facets of the Dhamma. We need only bear these teachings in mind and watch as the evidence accumulates in our own experience.

LEONA: That's fair, that's certainly fair. I'd say a certain amount has accumulated already. I can see that good and bad deeds have effects here in this present life, and if those effects go beyond, say to a future birth, well, I'm open-minded about the matter. Tell me this, please. These connections we were speaking of—do they exist between animals and human beings? Can human beings be reborn as animals and vice versa?

Bhikkhu Tissa and the Greater Good 51

BHIKKHU: We must first note that according to Buddhism there is no self or soul that is literally born again, but rather a chain of causes or a stream of life that springs up now here, now there, according to conditions. But in ordinary, conventional language we can certainly say that a human being can be reborn as an animal or vice versa. It all depends on the individual's kamma, his or her accumulated deeds.

LEONA: Ah, here we have the core of your opposition to cruelty to animals. We are related to them. We may even *become* them.

BHIKKHU: In the Buddhist view all sentient life is related. The differentiations are temporary, fluctuating, and merely provisional. Countless living beings go wandering through the endless cycles of *saṁsāra*, being born high or low, in this world or that, with much suffering or little suffering.

ERNEST: Hence the great Buddhist emphasis on compassion. Yes, I see. We are all part of an organic whole.

BHIKKHU: Yes, all sentient life is organic and inter-related, but you should not make the common, romantic mistake of thinking that this "whole" is *good*. *Saṁsāra* is, to one degree or another, suffering throughout, and we beings trapped in *saṁsāra* are suffering.

ERNEST: All the more reason for compassion, then!

BHIKKHU: Quite so. And here is a point of Dhamma I want to emphasize especially. One's own ultimate welfare and the welfare of other beings are perfectly harmonious. The life of moral restraint is a life of service to others, because it protects others, soothes them, and inspires them to similar effort. When we follow the path and strive to purify our minds we set incalculable reverberations going in the hearts of other beings. Never doubt that the Dhamma conduces to the greater good, even when circumstances seem to push us toward shabby expediency. The law of kamma sees to it that in the long run deeds work out according to their nature, so we should always take the wide view, always strive for detachment in our reflections, so that we can make wise choices.

ERNEST: If one lives as you suggest, being diligent in practising Dhamma, could one be reborn in a heavenly world, a world of bliss?

BHIKKHU: Yes, that's possible.

ERNEST: Wouldn't unadulterated bliss be as good as Nibbāna? Wouldn't that be the end of suffering?

BHIKKHU: No, the so-called heavenly worlds are not perfect refuges for two reasons. First, *all* worldly bliss is adulterated. There is suffering in even the highest realms. It is very fine and attenuated, but it exists. In the ultimate sense, pleasure itself is suffering, a dis-ease, a kind of irritation to the mind that deprives it of peace. The second reason is that even though life in those planes is said to be very pleasant and long, it is still impermanent: it is going to come to an end; it cannot be relied upon forever; hence there is anxiety and uncertainty even for beings living there.

LEONA: A flawed heaven. How gloomy!

BHIKKHU: Actually, this human world is considered an especially fortunate place to be born. The beings in higher realms are so drenched with pleasure that they have little inducement to strive for deliverance. And the animals and beings in the unhappy lower planes are too unintelligent or too miserable to make spiritual progress. This human world with its puzzling mixture of pleasure and pain often makes people think.

LEONA: Indeed it does that!

BHIKKHU: We really need not speculate about other planes of life when our own provokes us to search for liberation. And now, of course, though the world is full of misery, still we have the priceless treasure of the Dhamma, which the Buddha discovered and made known to cure suffering and free beings from the wheel of birth and death.

ERNEST: Bhikkhu Tissa, it seems the Dhamma is a very demanding teaching.

BHIKKHU: And we are demanding people, are we not? We demand pleasure and security and comfort—and we demand them to be permanent! This is impossible, of course, because the universe is not under our control. So we suffer. And then we demand an end to suffering, preferably through no exertion of our own. We want an escape from old age and illness and death, but, as the Buddha says, this cannot be got by mere wanting, and not to get what one desires, that is suffering, too.

ERNEST: True, true. We are indeed contrary creatures! I see the justice of what you say—we have to make an effort if we really want to accomplish anything. But the question I ask myself is, how much do I want to accomplish?

BHIKKHU: Nobody can answer that question but you.

ERNEST: Considering my limitations I sometimes wonder if I couldn't sort of stop half-way, as it were—just practise basic morality and try to live a modest life and keep out of trouble.

BHIKKHU: The way of Dhamma is a way that goes against the stream of the world and the world's desires. If you cease to struggle against the current, do you think you will just remain stationary?

ERNEST: Well, no, considering the nature of my mind.

LEONA: Going with the flow just won't make it, huh?

BHIKKHU: Going with the flow means succumbing to craving and clinging, which pull us down to suffering. It is said that the Dhamma protects the Dhammafarer. This means that one who resists craving and clinging, who makes an effort against the worldly stream, becomes stronger by that very effort, just as when we exercise a muscle we strengthen it. By overcoming even small problems with mindfulness and detachment we find ourselves increasingly able—and willing—to surmount spiritual obstacles. I think that if you try to apply the Dhamma in life you will quickly notice within yourself the growth of confidence.

ERNEST: There's something in that. I do feel some confidence—just a little bit!

BHIKKHU: The Buddha said that a follower should examine his teaching in the way that a goldsmith analyzes gold—carefully inspecting, refining, testing it before concluding that it is real. So if you have undertaken to practise the Dhamma even a little, then please reflect on the result of that practice and see how you feel about it, see whether you feel cheered and inspired to go a little further.

ERNEST: Here we are—Leona and I—offering a meal to a monk and listening to him preach—something I would have thought ridiculous a year ago! I guess that says something.

LEONA: To me, Bhikkhu Tissa, the Dhamma is appealing because it seems to satisfy both the intellect and the emotions. I've never been a religious person, mainly because I couldn't believe passionately in the supernatural. On the other hand, the materialistic philosophies leave me cold, because they have no understanding of the mind and what for lack of a better word I will call the transcendental. They are earthbound and infinitely depressing. Then there is the swarm of cults and quasi-religions which are *both* hysterical and intellectually incoherent. Whew! It's enough to make me an absolute agnostic. Except ... agnosticism is itself a blind belief! Now I've studied the Dhamma a little bit, and while I don't understand everything, I find it, well, refreshing. As I said, it fits together intellectually and it gives scope to the desire for transcendence, the impulse to become purer or wiser than we now are. Just this morning, before you came, I read a passage in one of Ernest's books that summarized the Dhamma as clear, visible, leading onward—something succinct like that.

BHIKKHU: "Well expounded is the Dhamma by the Exalted One, directly visible, immediately effective, calling one to come and see, leading onward, to be personally realized by the wise."

LEONA: That's it. As clear a statement as I've heard. Now, if it can fulfill that promise . . . .

BHIKKHU: The truths of the Dhamma are for us to examine and confirm. We have to remove the obstructions to our understanding by practising morality and training ourselves in the art of concentration. When the conscience is clear and the mind can hold steady on the objects of attention, then wisdom arises of its own nature. We don't create it.

ERNEST: But wisdom is not the end, is it?

BHIKKHU: No. Wisdom is the sword we use to cut off defilements, to clear a path for ourselves out of the jungle and into the open air.

ERNEST: Buddhism grants us immense freedom of action, doesn't it?

LEONA: And immense responsibility, it seems. If all planes of existence are somehow tied to suffering then probably we should use that freedom of action to get freedom . . . of being! Or I might say, if it is *possible* to escape suffering and gain enlightenment, then if we don't *try*, our misery would be really our own fault.

Bhikkhu Tissa and the Greater Good   57

ERNEST: What a predicament. Bhikkhu Tissa, you were right when you said that Buddhism challenges us.

BHIKKHU: The problem of existence and its solution are both contained within the Four Noble Truths. The truth of the omnipresence of suffering in *saṁsāra* and the truth of its arising out of craving point out our plight. The truth of the cessation of suffering and the truth of the way to accomplish that point out the escape from this plight. So you see, there is darkness and light—the darkness of pain and ignorance and confusion, and the light of understanding and deliverance. Life for the intelligent person should be a journey from dark to light.

ERNEST: But how long and how fast?

BHIKKHU: As long as it takes and as fast as you wish.

ERNEST: Well, it's a little frightening, but it's exhilarating, too. In time I might actually be able to make sense out of the universe! Already I feel a certain tension between my miserable old habits of mind and my urge to pursue the Dhamma further. It is sort of dazzling to think that I can walk down the street like anybody else but still be practising mindfulness, or still be reflecting on impermanence, suffering, and non-self. I wonder if I shouldn't be living in a cave or a jungle!

BHIKKHU: You'd still be dealing with the same mind in a cave, Ernest. Better to investigate in your own house—I mean, this very body and mind. The world is to be found there, and liberation from the world. Arising and passing away, suffering, and the empty, flickering personality can be seen and examined within. Wisdom isn't a treasure we can prospect for in the Himalayas; it appears only when conditions are right for it, when the mind is settled, not distracted.

LEONA: When I read the words of the Buddha I get a feeling of immense wisdom, and yet he doesn't answer some questions about the origin of the universe, about what happens to an enlightened person after death, and so on. Now, I'm sure he had good reasons for not answering what might be extraneous questions, but still ....

BHIKKHU: Never forget, Leona, that the Buddha was not out to build a reputation for himself, or to be a human computer spewing information, or to dazzle the ignorant with amazing secrets. He was out to cure suffering. He was a supreme genius, but he never lost sight of his practical purpose: to teach suffering and the way to the ending of suffering. He taught what was necessary. Whatever else he may have *known* it is useless to speculate about. Once, when the Buddha was seated in a forest with a company of monks, he took up a handful of leaves from the ground and showed them to the monks. He asked them which were more numerous, the leaves in his hand or the leaves in the entire forest. The monks reasonably noted that the leaves in his hand were very few compared to those in the entire forest. The Buddha then said that those in his hand were as the truths he had revealed to them, and those in the whole forest were as the truths he knew but had *not* revealed.

LEONA: And why hadn't he revealed them?

BHIKKHU: Because, the Buddha said, they were not useful, they did not lead to dispassion, to tranquility, to higher knowledge, to enlightenment. Remember, the Buddha had no need to teach at all. He had attained enlightenment, he was free, he had vanquished suffering. There was nothing further he needed to do. Yet he did act, he did exert himself. Why? Simply because of his all-embracing compassion. He taught his followers everything they needed to know about suffering and how to conquer it themselves. He held back nothing of value. Before he died he declared that as a teacher he had never had a "closed fist." He gave unstintingly of the Dhamma that pointed to liberation, entrusting it to his followers who have preserved it and honoured it and offered it as the supreme refuge for a weary world, even to this very day.

ERNEST: That's an encouraging thought. If the Buddha had no personal need to teach anything to anybody yet did teach for the rest of his life, then surely he thought that the teaching would be effective, that his followers, even though they weren't Buddhas, could still attain enlightenment through their own efforts.

BHIKKHU: Yes, indeed. The Buddha is sometimes called the great physician for the ills of the world. He doesn't cure by magic or laying on of hands or divine power. He prescribes for us the medicine of the Dhamma and instructs us in how to use it.

LEONA: But the patients have to be willing, don't they?

BHIKKHU: Oh yes. Some people complain about the emphasis on suffering in Buddhism; they prefer not to think about it. They suffer, they know they suffer, but they don't realize that suffering is a deep and terrible spiritual disease. Only when they take a close look at their situation do they feel moved to do something about it. It's like a man who smells smoke in his house. If he's intelligent he investigates and sees that his house is on fire. Rather than waiting to be burned, he looks around for an escape and makes use of it promptly—he climbs out a window and slides down the drain-pipe. What the Buddha teaches us first of all is that our house *is* on fire—on fire with greed, with hate, with delusion, burning with sickness, old age, death, lamentation, despair.

ERNEST: The truth of suffering, in short.

BHIKKHU: And then the Buddha points out the reasons for this suffering and what can be done about it and how there might be ease and relief for us instead of anxiety and pain. And, more than this, the Buddha shows how our lives may become calmer, wiser, and purer, and how we may in fact achieve what we hardly can imagine: enlightenment, a radiant and unassailable security.

LEONA (Sighing): It's a shame we are not living in the time of the Buddha himself.

BHIKKHU: Ah, but we are, Leona. We are! The Buddha says that whoever sees the Dhamma sees the

Bhikkhu Tissa and the Greater Good 61

Buddha. And the Dhamma is not only written in books, it is written in the elements of the world as well.

LEONA: What do you mean?

BHIKKHU: The three characteristics of existence —impermanence, suffering, and non-self—spring up everywhere for the benefit of the diligent meditator. Look at the flames there in the fireplace, snapping and curling and flickering in front of our eyes.

LEONA: Ah, impermanence, yes, of course.

BHIKKHU: Yes, both an instance and an emblem of the changing nature of reality.

ERNEST: Transience and change.

BHIKKHU: And more than that. Don't you see in those wavering sheets of fire and those sputtering little flames something futile and weary? They leap up, they fall back, they smoulder and fail.

ERNEST: An incompleteness, a restlessness. You might call it suffering!

BHIKKHU: And within that chemical reaction we call fire, within that shifting light and heat what's really going on? Is the fire one stable thing and the log another? Does the wood stay the same while the fire just happens to it?

LEONA: No, they're both changing, there's only change. The wood is always changing to something else. You could say it's not being, it's only *becoming*. Therefore....

ERNEST: Therefore it's not a self! Just non-self. Well, Bhikkhu Tissa, this is something. Even my own fireplace can instruct me in the Dhamma.

BHIKKHU: And why stop there? Out the window there we can see that it's snowing a little harder. There! See that swirl of wind? Look at the flakes spinning against the grayness. What do they suggest to you?

LEONA: Change. Impermanence. And then there's the sadness of it—I don't know why, it's just the wandering, the endless unease. We could call it suffering, sure. And as before, in that change, in that process, I don't see any persisting element. No self. Just like the fire.

BHIKKHU: Just like the fire. And yet the one is blazing hot and the other is icy cold. Still the same truths are manifest in both. Do you see the principle I am getting at?

LEONA: I think I do. All the world is food for contemplation.

BHIKKHU: And above all, do not neglect your own body and mind. That's where craving clings the tightest, that's where ignorance resides.

LEONA: You are assuming, of course, that I'll keep investigating the Dhamma.

BHIKKHU: I am assuming it.

LEONA (Smiling): Well, you're right, I guess. Can't quit now. I'll keep going a little further.

ERNEST: Going toward what, Leona?

LEONA: Why .... Let's call it the greater good, shall we?

ERNEST: Why not?

LEONA: It seems it's possible to live deliberately,

and if so, I think one ought to live for the benefit of oneself and others.

ERNEST: And others, yes. Speaking of that. Uh, Leona, talking to this venerable monk has made me sure that I don't want to—I mean, I couldn't possibly accept that job at the chemical company.

LEONA: Oh, Earnest. As for the job ....

ERNEST: No, really, you have to see—I just wouldn't feel ....

LEONA: Peace, husband of mine! There is no dispute.

ERNEST: Say what?

LEONA (Smiling, laying a hand on his arm): Under no circumstances can you accept that job. You are happy where you are. You don't want to be even distantly connected to the suffering of animals. I understand that now. I respect it. Venerable Tissa is skillful, I think, in nudging us in the direction of the Dhamma.

ERNEST: But you were so in favour of the job.

LEONA (Shrugging): Ah, well. Impermanence!

ERNEST: You're a remarkable woman, Leona.

LEONA: It depends on who's doing the remarking! But enough. Let's not weary this tolerant monk any more today, all right? Look, Ernest, the snow is coming down harder. Maybe you had better drive Venerable Tissa home.

ERNEST: You don't have a "home," do you, Bhikkhu Tissa? Just a monastery.

BHIKKHU: There's no real home for any of us short of Nibbāna. But yes, perhaps it's time to go.

ERNEST: Thank you for your time.

BHIKKHU: And thank you for your food.

LEONA: *You* are the one who's given real food, Bhikkhu Tissa.

ERNEST: We appreciate your teaching.

BHIKKHU: I'm glad you do. But the fire teaches, too. And the snow. And your own hearts.

ERNEST: Shall we go, then?

They rise. Bhikkhu Tissa, wrapped up in his robes, follows Ernest out the door into the sudden cold and light of the snowy day. Leona stands on the doorstep and watches them go down to the car. The wind gusts and the snow falls harder, blurring the landscape and the vanishing figures. At the car, Bhikkhu Tissa turns, smiles, and waves. Or does he wave? She is not sure. Maybe he has pointed at the chaos of snowflakes, or the invisible clouds, or the ghostly horizon of rooftops. Then the car rolls away. Leona stands gazing after for a moment. The world seems huge and full of silence. Snow-dust blows from the limbs of an oak.

ABOUT THE AUTHOR

Bhikkhu Nyanasobhano (Leonard Price), an American from Louisville, Kentucky, was ordained as a Buddhist monk at Wat Mahadhatu in Bangkok in 1987. He is the author of *Radical Buddhism* (BL 92), *To the Cemetery and Back* (BL 96), and *Bhikkhu Tissa Dispels Some Doubts* (BL 102), published under his civilian name; and *A Buddhist View of Abortion* (BL 117), published under his monastic name. A book of essays, *Living As A Buddhist,* awaits publication in the United States. Bhikkhu Nyanasobhano presently resides at Jetavana Vihara in Washington, D.C.

Now available from BPS

LIVING BUDDHIST MASTERS
Jack Kornfield

In the dozen years it has been in print, *Living Buddhist Masters* has proved to be one of the most valuable books on Theravada Buddhist practice ever published. Compiled by American Vipassana teacher Jack Kornfield, the book brings to the reader the precise instructions of twelve of the greatest meditation masters of our time. In their own words such teachers as Mahasi Sayadaw, Achaan Chah, Sunlun Sayadaw, U Ba Khin and others explain the way of practice that has led them and their students to the realization of the truths of the Dhamma. These masters show how alive Buddhist practice is in the monasteries of their countries and they invite the reader to understand and work directly with their ways of practice. Excellent introductory chapters by the compiler lucidly set out the basic framework of Buddhist practice and describe the settings of contemporary monasteries and masters in Thailand and Burma. Photographs of each of the masters are included.

320 pages *Price as in latest BPS catalog*
Softback   *ISBN 955-24-0042-2*

THE BUDDHIST PUBLICATION SOCIETY

is an approved charity dedicated to making known the Teaching of the Buddha, which has a vital message for people of all creeds. Founded in 1958, the BPS has published a wide variety of books and booklets covering a great range of topics. Its publications include accurate annotated translations of the Buddha's discourses, standard reference works, as well as original contemporary expositions of Buddhist thought and practice. These works present Buddhism as it truly is—a dynamic force which has influenced receptive minds for the past 2500 years and is still as relevant today as it was when it first arose. A full list of our publications will be sent free of charge upon request. Write to:

The Hony. Secretary
BUDDHIST PUBLICATION SOCIETY
P.O. Box 61
54, Sangharaja Mawatha
Kandy   Sri Lanka